MW00422947

THE PRACTICAL STRATEGIES SERIES
IN GIFTED EDUCATION

series editors
FRANCES A. KARNES & KRISTEN R. STEPHENS

Challenging
Highly Gifted Learners

Barbara Gilman

PRUFROCK PRESS INC.

Copyright ©2008 by Frances A. Karnes
and Kristen R. Stephens-Kozak

All rights reserved.

No part of this book may be reproduced, translated, stored in a retrieval system, or transmitted, in any form or by any means, electronic, mechanical, photocopying, microfilming, recording, or otherwise, without written permission from the publisher.

Printed in the United States of America.

ISBN-13: 978-1-59363-320-2
ISBN-10: 1-59363-320-3

At the time of this book's publication, all facts and figures cited are the most current available. All telephone numbers, addresses, and Web site URLs are accurate and active. All publications, organizations, Web sites, and other resources exist as described in the book, and all have been verified. The authors and Prufrock Press, Inc., make no warranty or guarantee concerning the information and materials given out by organizations or content found at Web sites, and we are not responsible for any changes that occur after this book's publication. If you find an error, please contact Prufrock Press, Inc. We strongly recommend to parents, teachers, and other adults that you monitor children's use of the Internet.

Prufrock Press, Inc.
P.O. Box 8813
Waco, Texas 76714-8813
(800) 998-2208
Fax (800) 240-0333
http://www.prufrock.com

Contents

The Practical Strategies Series in Gifted Education offers teachers, counselors, administrators, parents, and other interested parties up-to-date instructional techniques and information on a variety of issues pertinent to the field of gifted education. Each guide addresses a focused topic and is written by scholars with authority on the issue. Several guides have been published. Among the titles are:

- *Acceleration Strategies for Teaching Gifted Learners*
- *Curriculum Compacting: An Easy Start to Differentiating for High-Potential Students*
- *Enrichment Opportunities for Gifted Learners*
- *Independent Study for Gifted Learners*
- *Motivating Gifted Students*
- *Questioning Strategies for Teaching the Gifted*
- *Social & Emotional Teaching Strategies*
- *Using Media & Technology With Gifted Learners*

For a current listing of available guides within the series, please contact Prufrock Press at (800) 998-2208 or visit http://www.prufrock.com.

Savannah smiled graciously, her mature height and articulate speech disguising her relative youth. "I'm full time at the high school this year," she beamed, having begun the previous fall at age 12, after completing 40 credits of high school work while in middle school. Modifications to Savannah's education began in earnest in the fall of her fourth-grade year, when she revealed to her parents that she knew most of what was being taught and wished she could move ahead. In a subsequent meeting, her teachers tactfully admitted the quiet student showed no signs of needing advanced work, but individual assessment results told a different story. Savannah's highly gifted Wechsler IQ scores, near the ceiling of the test, and advanced achievement levels convinced a fifth-grade teacher at the meeting to let her visit his classroom. Savannah never left, immediately finding a more comfortable fit with older classmates and more advanced work. The teacher particularly supported her love of science with projects she shared with other gifted students.

The following year, working at home, Savannah completed Stanford University's Education Program for Gifted Youth (EPGY) math coursework through prealgebra, earning high grades. As her sixth-grade year was about to begin at school, she hoped for more advanced math and science, but wished to remain with the class she had joined in fifth grade. More confident now of her potential success, school personnel allowed her to take Algebra I with the eighth graders, skip sixth-grade science, and take seventh- and eighth-grade science concurrently. Savannah performed beautifully, even rejecting the thoughtful counselor's offer to create a "circle of friends" to ease her transition into the eighth-grade math class. She was fine, she assured him, and her algebra teacher had to agree.

In fact, Savannah was more than fine. She began to flourish and this introverted student gained confidence in her abilities. Soon, she was taking high school classes, happily challenging herself and blossoming in the process. Although not specifically designed for a highly gifted student, this patchwork of higher level classes met Savannah's needs well enough that she turned down the opportunity to attend a charter school for advanced students, preferring to stay with the friends she had made.

Unfortunately, in the midst of a decision about weighted grades, class rank, and the extreme competition to become valedictorian in some of the district's high schools, Savannah's local school board decided to eliminate the opportunity for any middle schooler to earn high school credit prior to entering high school full time. One official opined that the only reason he could imagine for a middle schooler to take high school classes would be to gain an early lock on becoming valedictorian. The student could thereby increase the number of weighted-grade classes beyond what a typical 4-year high school student could take and ensure the highest grade point average (GPA).

Of course, Savannah was unaware of such concerns. She simply wanted work that was satisfying and already had been embarrassed to accept even small honors in awards assemblies, stating *that* was not the reason she worked diligently. The school district compromised to allow Savannah to keep her course credits, but her top grades in those courses would not be used to compute her GPA. Now, she would have a less-than-typical chance of becoming valedictorian, with fewer weighted-grade classes and only the hardest ones left to take. At least she would be able to terminate her high school career earlier and move on.

Although Savannah's specific needs are unique, her general situation is not. In-class accommodations for the gifted rarely are adequate for the highly gifted child. Enrichment pull-outs also fail to address achievement levels several grades higher than a child's placement. Most highly gifted students require acceleration, either subject level or full grade, at various points in their education. When advanced, they typically do well and enjoy a better fit socially. Identifying their needs can be difficult without in-depth, individual assessment, especially because introversion is their dominant personality style (Silverman, 1998) and most hesitate to self-advocate. Finally, because the academic progression of highly gifted students is so unusual, a variety of rules and red tape developed for average students can frustrate their progress.

Savannah maintained her optimism, but many highly gifted children succumb to school difficulties. As a group, our most gifted students are not our highest achievers. Clinicians who work with the gifted know that the *moderately gifted* child (IQ 130), at two standard deviations above the mean, stands a better chance of experiencing satisfaction and performing optimally in typical schools than more highly gifted students. At three standard deviations above the mean (IQ 145), the *highly gifted* child may be the valedictorian but also may be the underachiever who feels like an outsider at school, ill-served by the course offerings available. At *exceptionally gifted* (IQ 160) and *profoundly gifted* (IQ 175) levels, student frustration escalates substantially with depression, underachievement, school drop out, and even the specter of suicide possible (Gilman, in press; Hately, 2007; Meckstroth, 2007). The child relates best to older children or teachers, not age peers, so finding true friends is difficult. Moreover, the highly, exceptionally, or profoundly gifted student learns so quickly that a typical, age-grade curriculum can exert a strangle hold, threatening the student's motivation to learn. At the same time, the student fails to learn solid study habits and organizational skills, because they are not yet needed, planting the seeds for potential failure in college or graduate school.

Miraca Gross' (2004a) longitudinal study of exceptionally gifted Australian students (160 IQ and up) found that those enrolled in typical school programs struggled to complete their education satisfactorily and find satisfying jobs. These most intelligent children were among the least successful when their unusual needs were not accommodated in school. What allowed them to succeed? Gross (2004b) found that when exceptionally gifted students were radically accelerated 3 or more years during their K–12 education, they did better. Most completed high school, bachelors', and even graduate degrees with excellent grades and went on to a variety of fascinating careers as young adults. A perhaps unexpected result was that they valued the social aspects of acceleration most. Without it, they felt trapped with other children with whom they had little in common.

Case studies of highly, exceptionally, and profoundly gifted children are filled with tales of extraordinary cognitive development, unusual accomplishments, and difficulty fitting in. The following describes their challenges:

> Giftedness is asynchronous development in which advanced cognitive abilities and heightened intensity combine to create inner experiences and awareness that are qualitatively different from the norm. This asynchrony increases with higher intellectual capacity. The uniqueness of the gifted renders them particularly vulnerable and requires modifications in parenting, teaching and counseling in order for them to develop optimally. (Columbus Group, 1991)

The higher the level of giftedness, the more help that is needed in turning a risky school experience into a successful one.

Just as Savannah's teachers had no idea the quiet fourth grader needed full-grade acceleration, many teachers struggle to determine the learning needs of highly gifted children. What degree of accommodation will challenge them appropriately and maintain their motivation to learn?

Individual Education Plans (IEPs) for developmentally delayed or learning-disabled students are decided with the aid of in-depth, individual intelligence and achievement testing. The same is needed for highly gifted children. Although most are assessed on IQ screeners (e.g., Cognitive Abilities Test, Raven's Progressive Matrices, SAGES-2, or Otis-Lennon School Ability Test), these reveal little more than whether a student is gifted or not gifted, and rarely provide clues that a child is highly, exceptionally, or profoundly gifted. Grade-based achievement testing in school also is inadequate to measure the sometimes extraordinary advancement of the highly gifted. Without individual assessment by a qualified examiner, teachers have no way of knowing how gifted a child is or how advanced he or she may be academically. Every effort should be made to have the school provide such assessment or have parents obtain private testing.

Table 1

Academic Progress of a Profoundly Gifted Child as Measured by Grade Equivalents

	PIAT-R Age 6-1	K-TEA (Brief Form) Age 7-9	K-TEA Age 8-10
Math	2.6	10.9	Math Application 11.3 Math Computation 10.7
Reading	3.2	8.5	Reading Comprehension > 12.9 Reading Decoding 10.8
Spelling	2.8	5.2	Spelling 10.9

Note: Peabody Individual Achievement Test–Revised = PIAT-R; Kaufman Test of Educational Achievement = K-TEA.

Consider young Ben, who began reading in Kindergarten and made rapid progress to chapter books in 4–6 weeks during a reading contest. Ben earned a score of 132, in the moderately gifted range, on the Cognitive Abilities Test (CogAT), when tested for his school's gifted program. However, private testing yielded a Wechsler Full Scale IQ score of 145 (highly gifted level) and a subsequent Stanford-Binet L-M (SBL-M) IQ score of 192 (profoundly gifted), administered after Ben hit the ceiling of the Wechsler at several points and required a test with a higher ceiling to assess the full range of his abilities. Ben also was privately assessed on three different individual achievement tests just prior to first grade, in the spring of second grade, and in the spring of third grade—covering fewer than 3 years. Although the test scores have limited comparability, his grade equivalents can be compared to gain an idea of Ben's progress (see Table 1).

At age 6-1, just prior to first grade, Ben was performing at the level of average second and third graders. By age 8-10 (third grade), performance was at the high school level in all areas assessed. Although Ben did not need to move directly to high school, he required placement where he could be truly challenged, not just placed in a class where he was far above the rest of the students.

Students who consistently score 2 or 3 years above their grade placement in most areas except spelling (some brilliant children cannot spell) are good candidates for full-grade acceleration, if they concur with the placement. Full-grade skips most often are done one year at a time and reevaluated when the need arises. Others need subject-area acceleration, or a combination of both. As an example, two young boys with remarkable math reasoning posed a challenge; the 6-year-old scored at the high school graduate level, and the 7-year-old at the level of graduate students. Both needed to begin more abstract math soon, studying formal algebra and geometry, in order to maintain their interest in mathematics. The substitution of a self-paced math program would be excellent for such students.

Fortunately, Ben's private testing documented an extreme need for advancement. He was profoundly gifted and learning basic skills very quickly. His achievement scores supported his highest IQ score. As a result, his second-grade teacher provided advanced literature with several creative projects related to the books, substituted higher level spelling lists, sent him to third grade for math, added an enrichment opportunity for fifth-graders to learn public speaking, and advanced his individual work in all group projects. These accommodations were highly successful. At the end of his second-grade year, Ben skipped comfortably to fourth grade, his motivation to learn intact. And, he concluded, "My teacher changed my life." Never before had Ben had the opportunity to do truly challenging work and stretch himself to meet his teacher's high expectations.

Individual Intelligence Testing

The gold standard for cognitive assessment is the comprehensive individual intelligence or IQ test. IQ tests are used to determine overall cognitive functioning, as well as strengths and weaknesses in verbal abstract reasoning and language, nonverbal and visual-spatial reasoning, and processing skills (short-term memory and speed on paper-and-pencil tests). The reasoning portions of the tests are better indicators of giftedness than the processing skills portions, on which gifted children tend to score somewhat lower (Flanagan & Kaufman, 2004; Gilman & Falk, 2005; Rimm, Gilman, & Silverman, 2008).

Current major IQ tests, such as the Wechsler Intelligence Scale for Children-Fourth Edition (WISC-IV), have ceiling limits of 150 to 160 for global scores (Wechsler, 2003). A highly gifted child usually can earn a score of 145+ in one of the areas recommended by the National Association for Gifted Children's (NAGC; 2008) position statement on use of the WISC-IV to document this ability: General Ability Index (GAI), Full Scale IQ (FSIQ), Verbal Comprehension Composite, or Perceptual Reasoning Composite. However, considerably higher levels of ability generally have been out of reach for such instruments, using standard normative scaling. When the child's scores cluster around the ceiling of the test, or the child answers the most difficult questions on subtests without reaching discontinue criteria, test scores likely will be underestimates of actual ability.

Ceiling Problems

How can high-scoring children, who represent a wide range of giftedness capped by an arbitrary ceiling, be further differentiated? Ratio-based scoring systems, like the Stanford-Binet L-M (SBL-M) utilizes, have been helpful in locating exceptionally and profoundly gifted children not found by tests with normative scaling (Rimm et al., 2008). Based on the original concept of an Intelligence Quotient (IQ = Mental Age ÷ Chronological Age ×100), they reflect what a child actually can do, compared with developmental expectations for a child of that age. Ratio-based scoring imposes no arbitrary ceiling; scores can rise above the 150s, sometimes exceeding 200. The only limitations are the child's age at testing and the difficulty level of the highest items, so the best estimates of ability are obtained in young children not yet able to answer the most difficult questions on the test. Using the SBL-M for young children, ideally age 9 or younger, helps to counteract the difficulty that development is not consistent.

A 5-year-old with a mental age of 10 makes more sense than a 15-year-old with a mental age of 30.

Riverside Publishing still allows use of its 1972 Stanford-Binet L-M (Terman & Merrill, 1973) as a retest, when children score near the ceiling of a current test (Carson & Roid, 2004). The SBL-M remains an excellent measure of advanced reasoning with a high ceiling (Superior Adult III level). As recently as 2005, in a special testing forum at the World Council for Gifted and Talented Children, Dr. Richard Boolootian, of the Mirman School in Los Angeles, noted that the SBL-M had always correctly identified students for Mirman, a school for the highly gifted. He wondered what new measures could adequately replace it (Boolootian, 2005). Many examiners continue to use the SBL-M because it yields scores that fit other observed advancement in these unusual children.

The SBL-M does not "always score higher," as some critics allege; retesting will yield a full range of scores from about the same to far higher, clearly differentiating the group that scored within a small range on a previous test. Concerns about its scoring too high because the population is growing more intelligent, a phenomenon referred to as the Flynn effect (Flynn, 1984, 1987), recently have been countered by indications the Flynn effect no longer applies to industrialized nations (Teasdale & Owen, 2005; Wasserman, 2007). If anything, today's children score a bit lower than they might have in 1972 due to several outdated questions most miss.

Fortunately, interest has been growing among test authors and psychologists to develop new strategies to differentiate the highly gifted on current instruments. Gale Roid, author of the Stanford-Binet Intelligence Scale-Fifth Edition (SB5, 2003b) has added several scoring options for gifted children (Roid & Carson, 2004). Among them, the Rasch-ratio score uses change-sensitive scores in a similar comparison of test ages with chronological age. Roid (2003a) noted that this metric allows criterion-referencing to task complexity and age-related skill development, which is relevant when planning programs for children likely to need acceleration. Psychologist Sylvia Rimm (2006) has suggested a similar Rimm-Ratio score for the WISC-IV, using the Test/Age Equivalents published in the manual, and comparing them with chronological age.

In 2007, The Psychological Corporation (PsychCorp) agreed to extend the scoring ceiling on the WISC-IV after the NAGC Task Force on IQ Test Interpretation (assembled in 2006 by Sylvia Rimm) provided research on more than 300 gifted children tested. Many earned WISC-IV raw score points well beyond the minimum needed to achieve the test's highest subtest scaled scores and global scores. Based on these results, PsychCorp agreed to further extend subtest scaled scores originally capped at 19 (99.9th percentile) to as high as 28 on some subtests for some ages, and global scores (GAIs, FSIQs, and composite scores) to as high as 210.

On November 9, 2007, Dr. Tom Cayton, Senior Director of Psychological Test Development at the PsychCorp, informed the task force that these extended norms, based on a smooth extension of the test's normative scaling, were complete. They were subsequently offered online (Zhu, Cayton, Weiss, & Gabel, 2008). The extended norms will ensure more accurate scoring for children who earn at least two scaled scores of 18 (99.6th percentile), and will especially help those who earn several 19s, with a number of raw score points beyond the minimum needed to yield that highest scaled score. However, task force members have noted that the extended norms will not document higher abilities for children who score just short of this requirement, failing to meet discontinue criteria on a number of subtests. Some members of the task force had tested children who answered many of the most difficult items on the tests, missing a few now and then, and failed to reach discontinue criteria for, perhaps, 7 of 10 subtests! These children's abilities were likely to be beyond the limits of the test, but the extended scoring would not confirm it. Even with such limitations, the WISC-IV extended norms can begin to document the abilities of children who need educational programs or support groups for the exceptionally and profoundly gifted.

All such assessment approaches further differentiate highly gifted students and find children who are truly at risk due to extraordinary advancement. Testers will need to seek out current available information on such techniques, which have been developed since major test manuals were originally distributed. They are important advancements and can aid program planning and provide educators willing to make unusual accommodations documented support for doing so. Table 2 summarizes the major tests and their advantages/disadvantages for highly gifted assessment.

If the child performs as expected and the test has an adequate ceiling, it may be given only once. IQ testing need not be repeated at regular intervals for a *current* estimate. Highly gifted children may reach test ceilings early, so scores earned when they are younger usually offer the best estimate of ability.

Measuring Achievement

Individual Achievement Tests

When extraordinary advancement is a possibility, students require an individual achievement test that samples abilities at many grade levels, not just a grade-level test. Such major achievement tests include the Woodcock-Johnson III NU Tests of Achievement (WJ III NU), Wechsler Individual Achievement Test, Second Edition (WIAT-II), and Kaufman Test of Educational Achievement: Second Edition (KTEA-II Comprehensive or Brief Form). Test ceilings vary, so a test having a ceiling similar to the child's IQ scores should be selected to ensure an accurate measurement of the child's achievement.

The combination of individual intelligence and achievement testing provides a road map for how quickly the student might be expected to progress and where current instruction should begin.

Table 2
Individual IQ Tests

Intelligence Test	Best Ages	Gifted Testing Considerations
Wechsler Intelligence Scale for Children, 4th ed. (WISC-IV)	6-0 through 16-11 (for gifted, use WAIS-III at 16)	Excellent first diagnostic test, often requested by schools. Nice verbal/visual-spatial balance, plus processing speed and memory. Higher "ceiling" than prior editions. GAI is usually best global indicator of giftedness. Substitute Arithmetic for a Working Memory subtest. Use PsychCorp's extended norms, if applicable, or add Rimm Ratios for additional information.
Wechsler Adult Intelligence Scale, 3rd ed. (WAIS-III)	16-0 through adult	Excellent adult diagnostic test (no higher IQ tests possible due to age). Verbal/visual-spatial balance, plus memory and processing speed. Use to document the need for accommodations for twice-exceptional students.
Wechsler Preschool and Primary Scale of Intelligence, 3rd ed. (WPPSI-III)	Ages 2-6 through 3-11 or Ages 4-0 through 7-3 (use WISC-IV at 6)	Strong, child-friendly, early test of verbal/visual reasoning, some fine-motor skills, general language. Useful for gifted school/program entrance.
Stanford-Binet Intelligence Scale, 5th ed. (SB5)	2-0 through adult	Strong test of math and visual-spatial reasoning (verbal abstract reasoning is limited), plus memory. A score of 120+ (not 130) on Verbal or Nonverbal Composite indicates giftedness. Consider scoring options: Rasch Ratio, Roid Gifted, and Nonverbal Composites. Pair with SBL-M for better verbal coverage.

Test	Age Range	Description
Stanford-Binet Intelligence Scale—Form L-M (SBL-M)[a]	2-0 through 9+ (for assessment of highly gifted)	Excellent reasoning test with less emphasis on processing skills. Used as a retest to differentiate higher levels of giftedness following high scores on another test. Features a normed ratio-based metric and very high scoring ceiling when used with younger children.
Differential Ability Scales (DAS) (Newer edition under review.)	6-0 through 17-11	Offers verbal, nonverbal, and spatial IQ scores and untimed spatial reasoning. Has a fairly high ceiling. Use the WAIS-III to document learning disabilities for ages 16–17.
Woodcock-Johnson III Tests of Cognitive Ability (WJ III Cog)	2-0 through adult	Diagnostically useful with gifted/learning-disabled children. Emphasizes processing skills heavily. Gifted children may earn lower scores.
Naglieri Nonverbal Abilities Test (NNAT);	5-0 through 17-11	Tests of visual abstract reasoning and pattern recognition. Useful for children with visual-spatial strengths, culturally diverse backgrounds, hearing deficits, speech/language issues, or limited English. Avoid as sole test where high verbal abilities exist.
Raven's Progressive Matrices: Coloured, Standard, Advanced;	5-0 through adult	
Universal Nonverbal Intelligence Test (UNIT)	5-0 through 17-11	

[a] This test with 1972 norms is approved by the publisher for exploring higher levels of giftedness in younger children following near-ceiling performance on a test with current norms.

Talent Searches

Talent Searches utilize college-board exams as out-of-level testing for younger children to assess unusual aptitude without ceiling problems. High scores on such exams, typically administered in seventh grade, qualify many students for educational programs with Duke University's Talent Identification Program (Duke TIP), the Johns Hopkins University Center for Talented Youth (CTY), Northwestern University's Center for Talent Development (CTD), the Rocky Mountain Academic Talent Search at the University of Denver, and other colleges, and high scores on out-of-level tests also suggest the need to review school placements.

Casual Assessment

Informal classroom assessment augments formal assessment and may be the only information available until individual testing is undertaken. Elementary teachers can casually assess reading, determining the level at which the student is suitably challenged, but not overwhelmed. Keep in mind, some highly gifted young children will pretend not to read, or read haltingly, if they perceive they should not be reading yet (Gilman, in press; Silverman, 2003). A writing prompt can sample written expression and explore a child's level of detail, descriptiveness, and creativity when writing. It also should be noted that some very gifted children may carefully reproduce the level of writing the teacher expects the other children to do (Gilman, in press).

Math knowledge can be explored with materials at different levels placed on a table, asking the child, "What is too easy?" "What is too difficult?" and "What is about right for you?" A meeting with the child's parents can determine what is being accomplished at home. Does the student have a chemistry lab, write poetry, or do mental multiplication? Encourage parents to keep portfolios of work and pictures of projects.

Middle or high school students can provide essays or creative writing and a list of classes taken and books read to help determine current instructional level. Prize-winning science projects, art, or published writing may clarify level of advancement.

Educational Plans for Highly Gifted Learners in School

Elementary Plans

Creating a brief written plan (Individual Learning Plan, Personal Learning Plan, Individual Education Plan) is a necessity to set learning goals for the highly gifted student during the school year. A meeting between parents and the teacher to discuss needs should be held as soon as possible in the fall. If parents have individual test reports, they should be shared with the classroom teacher immediately. If not, they should be encouraged to seek testing to document needs. The teacher may want to casually assess the child following the meeting to gain additional information before plans are finalized. Including the student for at least part of the meeting is important to gain his or her perspective and help in constructing effective learning plans. The primary goal of establishing the plan is to teach the highly gifted child at his or her actual level. Highly gifted children usually are both quite advanced and learn more quickly, so the plan is a device to set goals for doing the best job that is reasonably possible for a busy classroom teacher. The plan need not be perfect. It is the "best guess" of what would meet the child's needs. It can be brief, and there will be things in the regular curriculum that need not be changed. Once the plan is established, quarterly meetings should be held during the year to assess progress and make needed changes. The child may pace more quickly through planned material than anticipated or be unable to attend an enrichment experience in the building. The plan always should be considered a work in progress.

No discussion of individualized plans for the highly gifted can ignore accelerative options, either subject-area or full-grade, as these are critical accommodations for the highly gifted. Educators and parents should read the Templeton National Report on Acceleration—*A Nation Deceived: How Schools Hold Back America's Brightest Students* (Colangelo, Assouline, & Gross, 2004), available online at http://www.nationdeceived.org. It is important to note that *acceleration* is a misnomer because students are not pushed ahead. They are simply given access to instruction at their actual level. In fact, the first consideration in creating a plan is determining whether the student already is too advanced for the class. If a child is advanced well beyond grade placement (at least 2 years) in all areas except spelling, full-grade acceleration may be the best option, if the child concurs.

If the student is not so uniformly advanced or is too worried about leaving friends to consider a full-grade skip, an individualized plan can make the year worthwhile. When planning, the more advanced, appropriate work should be *substituted* for work that is too easy. If highly gifted children are required to do all of the regular work with their classmates and only given the option to do advanced work "in addition to" such work, they will stop choosing to do it.

A good place to start is with the subject area in which the child is most advanced or passionate. If advanced needs can be met by sending the child to a higher grade level for that particular subject, subject acceleration is an option that ensures continuous instruction at a higher level and does not require valuable teacher planning time every week. This is especially helpful with a more sequential subject, such as math or a foreign language, which would require considerable time to plan and teach individually.

If an accelerative option is chosen, a welcoming higher-grade-level teacher must be found to take the child, assuming the regular classroom teacher maintains primary responsibility for the student and works out the details. The child also must concur with this placement for it to be successful, so it is helpful to allow the student time to visit the advanced class and make a decision. Allow 30 days to be sure the placement is comfortable. The student can return to the original class, without any criticism, if things are not going well.

If subject-area acceleration is undertaken in this way, it is usually quite successful. The student quickly makes friends with older classmates and feels comfortable with two classes—a distinct advantage if full-grade acceleration is needed the next year. Moreover, this accommodation can be accomplished quickly, supporting the child's interest and allaying parent concerns about how the year will unfold.

If unusual needs can be accommodated within the classroom without acceleration, what options exist? Will the child's advanced reading be supported by the highest grade-level reading group or can individualization be done relatively easily by the classroom teacher? Several alternate books can be chosen, instead of the regular classroom selections, with literature study requiring more abstract reasoning about the characters, plot, and the like. The Junior Great Books program offers an excellent model for literature study, and sometimes a parent is willing to lead a group. Is the child a wonderful writer who would enjoy creative writing assignments? Can the child who is wild about science be allowed to do special science projects or be connected with a teacher who has a saltwater aquarium? The avid speller easily can be accommodated by substituting more advanced spelling lists and adding any words misspelled on the pretest taken by all students.

Because highly gifted children learn quickly, curriculum compacting is a helpful model to employ. Pretest before teaching and exempt the child from concepts already understood.

Allow the student to learn new material with less drill and practice. With the time saved, arrange projects of interest. These can address special topics the student enjoys and should be of greater depth and breadth than is typical for the grade level. If research skills have not yet been learned, they need to be taught. Help the child learn how to research answers to questions or interview helpful experts. There is no way teachers can answer all of the questions highly gifted children ask, but they can empower students to find the answers themselves.

Some parents are willing to provide a tutor for a subject in which the student is advanced, or utilize computer-based instruction with some schools even paying for this. Encourage any options that are reasonable and weave them into the child's school day. For example, EPGY, CTY, and Duke TIP offer instructional math programs designed for gifted children that allow students to work at their own pace, which is a distinct advantage. If the program is being provided by parents, math lessons can be viewed at home with homework done at school during the regular instructional time.

When the school refuses further advancement, some parents choose partial homeschooling. Usually they teach the advanced subjects at home and have the child attend school for art, music, P.E., and other subjects that are school strengths. When such situations present themselves, a helpful teacher can augment at school what is being done at home. Supporting the student's unusually fast progress, such programs recognize and support unique learning needs.

What if the school has established gifted programming, but it does not fit the highly gifted child's needs? The downside of schools becoming more aware of gifted needs and identifying children more universally is that some have special gifted classes at a predetermined level, rather than planning the programming each year to meet a specific student's needs. Such programs that extend the curriculum minimally but do not accelerate it (e.g., resource room programs) are convenient but do not properly address the needs of many gifted children, especially the highly gifted. When such programming is useful for a highly gifted child, perhaps a program designed for older children, it can be included in the learning plan. However, the teacher should not hesitate to look elsewhere to meet the unique needs of the highly, exceptionally, and profoundly gifted.

Finding several options for the learning plan to meet major needs can go a long way toward making the highly gifted student's year successful. Because the student is working at an appropriate level, good work habits and study skills are learned naturally. As the year ends, it is important to plan the next steps for the coming year. If the child completed accelerated work, a natural progression should follow next year. Avoid having the child repeat the same work next year "just to make sure there aren't any gaps in the child's education" or to stay with age peers. The few gaps highly gifted children encounter usually can be filled within hours, not school years, and few miss time with age peers when they are more comfortable with older children.

Middle and High School Plans

An individualized plan can benefit the older, highly gifted student who needs unusual accommodations or exemption from typical rules. When students have multiple teachers and classes, planning emphasizes access to higher level classes earlier, rather than within-class modifications. A knowledgeable counselor or principal can arrange for the student to elect advanced courses. Can the student skip an entry-level course? Can a middle schooler substitute a high school class, or can the high school student take college classes concurrently? Highly gifted students usually find advanced classes more appropriate, and enjoy both the older classmates and teachers with stronger specialization in a subject. They also appreciate the less authoritarian structure of college, with gentler attendance rules and fewer daily homework assignments they do not need. In addition, certain options can allow students to earn a high school diploma and bachelor's degree simultaneously.

Computer-based or online classes for the gifted also may be utilized. For example, Duke TIP offers AP courses for younger students, which might become part of the student's high school plan. Stanford's EPGY offers a full high school program. If possible, allow highly gifted middle and high school students to take more challenging courses and exempt them from less relevant classes and rules that are of little to no benefit to their educational needs.

The plan also may offer credit for internships, mentorships, or independent study. Such options can be especially effective for an underachieving, highly gifted student who might drop out of school. They support the student's interests and offer a needed opportunity to demonstrate talent in a different setting. If satisfying enough, such experiences can fuel the student's interest in completing school successfully.

The individualized plan documents such choices and serves as a contract, signed by the principal, in case of personnel changes. Students have found themselves in awkward positions when a principal transfers or retires, and the new administrator has a different view of what should be undertaken.

If the highly gifted student is doing advanced work, he or she should be given credit for it. A policy restricting high school credit to full-time high school students forces the truly advanced student to either stay too long in middle school or skip full grades to arrive at high school earlier than might be comfortable. Such policies ignore the needs of gifted students to progress commensurate with ability and cannot be recommended. As many successfully enter college early, the ramifications of offering early credit to such students are perfectly acceptable and prevent some from quitting high school to terminate unacceptable situations.

Without classroom modifications, can extracurricular enrichment satisfy needs? Generally, no. Highly gifted students are at risk because they spend too much time being held back in the regular classroom. They hear much more explanation and complete much more work than they need to grasp concepts.

Everything is too slow for them, they rarely encounter anything difficult, and they have no reason to develop good work habits or organizational skills. The natural curiosity that characterized them as young children wanes and they begin to lose interest in school. Essentially they are taught day after day to underproduce, and they can lose their motivation to learn.

The only effective way to prevent this is to modify their daily curriculum. Teach them at a higher level, increase the depth and breadth of their studies, and allow them to move on when they have learned concepts. When highly gifted students are presented with difficult challenges and work that engages them, they work harder, organize themselves, and learn how to avoid meltdowns when an answer is not initially obvious. They become better students and begin to realize their full potential. After all, isn't this what school is designed to do?

Clearly some teachers prove challenging for highly gifted students without changing their classroom procedures. The long-time AP English teacher, who heads the high school English department, and expects more of every student than he or she feels capable of producing, may teach at just the right level. The middle school science teacher who plans experiments she taught freshmen in college and produces more science fair winners than any other teacher in the district may be a good choice. The algebra teacher who is known for being difficult, and who taught many of the mathematically talented students in the district, will probably be fine. But, highly gifted students may need such teachers at younger ages and will need significant accommodations when placed in most classrooms.

With the pressure of state tests emphasizing high levels of competence with grade-level work, there may be fewer opportunities to teach some students differently and more fear of failing to prepare them properly for the tests if their work is altered. However, an emphasis on grade-level work for highly gifted children with advanced achievement levels is dangerous. It would be better to grade skip such students and expose them to more advanced work and testing than to hold them back. They rise to the occasion.

Family Preferences

When parents first become aware their children are highly gifted, the educational ramifications can be frightening. "I don't want my child in college at age 10!" is a common concern. Although the educational progress of highly gifted children can result in a shortened K–12 education, it need not lead to options parents resist.

Because it is virtually impossible to predict the future experience of the highly gifted child in school, it is unwise to plan far ahead. The best planning is done year-by-year, involves the child and teachers, and reviews current progress and options as they are needed. When this is accomplished, only the options children and their families view as helpful are chosen. Highly gifted students are quite careful about accelerative decisions, sometimes making choices to ensure a particular teacher, remain with friends, or even get their driver's license before proceeding to college. Each brings his or her own values to the decisions. For students who graduate early and enter college younger, choices still exist. Some attend colleges for high-school-aged students. Many attend regular universities, but live at home, live in a dorm close to home, or live in a dorm in another city with a parent moving nearby. Parents create the solutions they need.

Social Development: How Important Is Placement With Age Peers?

The Stanford-Binet L-M provides a mental age that is a remarkably good indicator of the level of a child's thinking, and the age of children he or she chooses for friends. Parents often report that the 6-year-old with a mental age of 10 routinely chooses to play with the 10-year-olds in the neighborhood—and is accepted. In contrast, the same 6-year-old probably struggles to find common interests with same-age peers. Highly gifted 6-year-olds tend to speak like adults, play more complicated games, and adhere to rules more than their classmates. They have trouble interacting with their same-age peers because they are thinking on a different plane.

Many educators believe that social development requires placement with same-age peers, but gifted children show little evidence of this. When they develop social skills, it is within the context of friendships, which occur with *true peers*—those with similar interests and thinking. Such children are usually either gifted or older. The highly gifted tend to value friends of all ages. They especially like adults and older children and may be quite protective and caring about younger children. Same-age peers present the greatest social challenge.

When highly gifted children are accelerated and placed with older classmates, they typically do very well. And, they maintain a variety of opportunities to spend time with same-age peers when they enroll in community athletic leagues, Boy or Girl Scouts, swim lessons, or age-based enrichment classes.

Highly Gifted Twice-Exceptional Learners

If giftedness is defined as *asynchronous development*, then the highly gifted student with disabilities may be the most asynchronous. It is destabilizing to have both extraordinary reasoning strengths and weaknesses. The child may be viewed as "so smart," yet struggle to learn skills other children master with ease. Highly gifted, twice-exceptional learners may come to doubt their intelligence. Even worse, high levels of giftedness mask subtle disabilities. The child may seem "smart, but lazy," with underachievement the only indication of a problem. Being labeled a student who "doesn't listen," "doesn't try," or is "unmotivated to learn" has negative ramifications that compound over time. Distinguishing the highly gifted child who underachieves for lack of challenge from the highly gifted student who struggles with disabilities is important.

For those with deficits, optimal teaching supports their *strengths* first, while gently accommodating their *weaknesses*. Twice-exceptional learners should be taught at their level of reasoning with accommodations made for any weaknesses. If highly gifted students are held back to the level of their weaknesses, and teaching only emphasizes those weak areas, these students may lose heart and resist school altogether. One exception would be when a child is struggling academically and undertaking therapeutic interventions, which can be exhausting. In such cases, it may be better to complete interventions, note improvement, and wait for confidence to increase before placing the child in more challenging situations. A delicate balance is needed, with strengths and favorite activities supported liberally, especially while therapies are underway. Such children will become late bloomers, but they will bloom.

Individual IQ testing reveals clues of disabilities, but an observant teacher may note subtle problems in the classroom. If a student fails to hear or understand verbal instructions; inadvertently drops to a lower line while reading; or is easily overloaded by the sounds, lights, and activity in the classroom—these all can be indications of deficits that should be further investigated. Brock and Fernette Eide (2006) explored common disabilities in *The Mislabeled Child*.

Specialists can best evaluate such students and suggest accommodations for the classroom. Behavioral optometrists (see http://www.covd.org) have special training in visual processing and can prescribe vision exercises for children with tracking problems, difficulties changing focus from near-point to far, and those who struggle with visual abstract patterns (Silverman, 2001). Children with a history of chronic ear infections often have auditory processing problems, which should be assessed by an audiologist (Silverman, 2002). They may have difficulty with background noise, experience delay in comprehending auditory information, be hypersensitive to loud sounds, or mishear words. These children need preferential seating, written instructions, and strategies to ensure they hear what is necessary. Children prone to sensory overload often benefit from occupational therapy for sensory processing disorder (see http://www.spdnetwork.org) and accommodations so they can calm themselves and regroup. Some highly gifted children exhibit Attention Deficit/Hyperactivity Disorder (ADHD)-like behaviors, but further assessment is needed to tease apart symptoms that can occur due to a lack of challenge in the classroom, auditory processing problems, or actual ADHD. Distractible highly gifted students may need particular help with organizational skills. Hyperactive highly gifted children may need opportunities for movement and can benefit from a very challenging, fast-paced academic program that encourages consistent engagement.

Handwriting difficulties are a common problem seen in gifted children, especially boys (Gilman, in press; Silverman, 2002), and are one of the easiest to address. Many struggle to write because their hands cannot keep up with their minds. If vision or sensory issues are to blame, treatment may help. However, all students benefit from learning to keyboard early, so composition skills are not delayed by reluctance to write. In the meantime, teachers can shorten writing assignments, while expecting top-notch work, and offer other avenues for the student to show what he or she knows (e.g., oral testing, PowerPoint presentations, dictation, creative projects). Holding such a highly gifted child back to the level of his or her handwriting until this "foundational skill" is mastered only seems to ensure a dislike of school.

Some of the most challenging disabilities also can coexist with high levels of giftedness. Consider 8-year-old Joshua. He was privately assessed because his visual difficulties (20/800 uncorrected) and dyslexic-like reading tendencies were difficult to accommodate at school without undermining his confidence. He wore glasses and was undergoing vision therapy in the hope of improving his vision as much as possible before having surgical correction in adulthood. Joshua grasped phonics, but struggled with reversals, and had problems sequencing letters into words, having to rely on mnemonic devices to spell. He also struggled with math and writing but was an excellent problem solver; critical thinker; gifted singer and actor; and creative producer of stories, songs, and exhibits. His oral expression far exceeded his written expression. Handwriting was laborious and frustrating for Joshua. He participated in a gifted literature resource program at his school, and his mother scribed for his writing assignments. "His writing is creative, insightful, with excellent word play," she wrote. Basic computation and number sense were difficult, and he struggled to tell time. Third grade brought an increase in math tests, spelling tests, and more worksheets. He had worked hard and earned mostly A's, but his mother worried about "keeping his intellectual self-esteem intact as he learns and is tested on the mechanics."

Private assessment documented extraordinary strengths, even higher than anticipated and dramatic weaknesses. A WISC-IV yielded scores in Verbal Comprehension (verbal reasoning and language) of 144 (99.8th percentile), Perceptual (visual) Reasoning of 117 (87th percentile), Working Memory of 102 (55th percentile), and Processing Speed of 78 (7th percentile). Joshua's verbal reasoning subtest scores, at the 98th, 99th and 99.9th percentiles suggested abilities beyond the limits of the WISC-IV, so the SBL-M was administered. Joshua earned a 176+ (profoundly gifted level) on the SBL-M, the plus added because he failed to reach a ceiling on the test and scored at the highest level. What should be done with a profoundly gifted child with such serious deficits?

Joshua had probably a six-standard-deviation discrepancy between his verbal reasoning and his weak handwriting and processing speed. Joshua qualified for a special education individual education plan (IEP), which needed to address both his physical disabilities related to vision (visual-motor coordination, speed of processing visual and visual-motor information) *and* his profoundly gifted reasoning ability and astronomical potential. His test report noted, "If he is taught to the level of his disabilities, he will never actualize his potential and his self-esteem will diminish. He must be taught to the level of his reasoning, with accommodations for his disabilities."

Joshua's school was on the right track including him in gifted literature study with his mother scribing for him. Additional recommendations were also made.

1. Joshua's IEP should include at least the following provisions:

   a. No timed tests or partial tests. When the time comes, Joshua will need double the amount of time for his college-board examinations or the maximum amount.
   b. Whatever Joshua can finish in class work or homework, in the amount of time it would take the majority of students to do the entire assignment, should be graded as the full assignment with no points lost.
   c. Give Joshua the hardest items to do, one-third as many as the other students.
   d. All assignments should be done on a keyboard, preferably with assistive technology that provides auditory feedback.
   e. All report card items related to spelling, processing speed, eye-hand coordination, and visual tasks should be marked "N/A," so that he does not suffer wounded self-esteem from his disabilities.
   f. All assignments should be graded on the basis of his conceptualization, not mechanics (spelling, punctuation, etc.), which are visual.
   g. A scribe will be necessary until Joshua develops sufficient processing speed so that he can complete his assignments on a keyboard.
2. Allow Joshua access to gifted programs usually reserved for older children such as robotics, chess club, and any offerings that become available.
3. Interventions and accommodations for weaknesses will, over time, lead to accelerated academic progress. Monitor Joshua's learning closely and offer advanced placements where needed. Acceleration (subject or full-grade) may be needed at various points in his education, as well as a variety of enrichment options.
4. Retest on the WJ-III NU Tests of Achievement at 1½ to 2½ year intervals as an aid to placement decisions.

Educators need to know that highly gifted students with disabilities can succeed. One young woman, Emma, with serious dyslexia and sequencing deficits, spent her elementary years in the learning-disabled track of a private school and did not test at the gifted level until age 13. Accepted to a self-contained gifted high school program, she had several primary accommodations: extra time for reading, books on tape, and written work graded for content not spelling. Emma won numerous academic awards in high school and went on to college, continuing to flourish with reading and writing adaptations (e.g., her parents were allowed to check e-mailed compositions for spelling errors that spell checker failed to recognize). Emma became an excellent reader, but her speed remained slow enough that a heavy college reading load was taxing.

Sometimes such students need to take fewer courses to ensure high-quality work without burning out. However, like Emma, many are finding help in assistive technology. As text readers and voice-activated word processors improve, the major impediments such students face will disappear, and their powerful ability can be fully expressed.

The Importance of Flexible School Personnel

Because highly gifted students have unique learning needs and are rarely understood, they encounter gatekeepers in school. Some insist the regular school program will be "just fine," enforce rules that do not make sense for these students, refuse requests for more advanced work or harder classes, focus on their weaknesses, lament the fact that any change for them will create a precedent, and effectively push them out of school. Educators can take a more positive, proactive role!

School personnel who think flexibly can create wonderful options for highly gifted students and have the fun of doing so. A perfect program is not essential. A plan that is responsive and respectful of the student's needs is. Armed with some information about education for the highly gifted, acceleration is usually positive, older classmates are preferred, and any gaps in knowledge easily can be filled. Passion-driven learning is the most compelling. Gifted students are willing to work hard if it is the *right* work. A patchwork of acceptable options can be assembled. When options to teach the highly gifted student at his or her level are allowed, families are grateful, students are motivated, and schools can proudly acknowledge their students' sometimes amazing accomplishments.

Ensure the following for any highly gifted student:

- individualized planning,
- access to advanced material,
- a faster instructional pace,
- continuous progress,
- opportunities to reason abstractly and think critically,
- access to true peers, and
- a supportive environment.

Place highly gifted elementary students with teachers who will have lots of ideas for teaching them. Consider accelerative opportunities to ensure continuous progress and motivate students. Plan with parents and the student to select middle and high school courses, basing placement on current achievement. Allow outside instruction to substitute for coursework in the building, when it seems reasonable. Many highly gifted students will perform better if they enter college early; some will even leave high school without diplomas.

Schools need not have extensive gifted programs to address such needs. A principal, counselor, district administrator, or school superintendent who wants to support a highly gifted student, and is willing to do some out-of-the-box thinking, can succeed. What could be better than advising a brilliant student, allowing some unusual options, and watching him or her flourish?

Being That Wonderful Teacher of the Highly Gifted

When learning needs are extreme, the classroom teacher can make a huge difference by making an ill-fitting curriculum relevant. Simply appreciating and supporting the student goes a long way. What should teachers remember when dealing with highly gifted students?

- *Giftedness is neither high achievement nor good citizenship.* Highly gifted students may not be motivated learners when the curriculum is a poor fit. Teaching them at their level is just good teaching, not a reward for proper behavior or perfect class work.
- *Individual assessment is critical to clarify needs and support unusual accommodations.* A comprehensive IQ test and an individual achievement test, with further testing to differentiate higher levels of giftedness if needed, can aid placement decisions. If a child's school cannot provide it, private assessment should be sought.
- *Expect enhanced gifted personality traits.* Sensitivity, intensity, perfectionism, concern with injustice, moral sensitivity, compassion, and questioning of authority abound, in addition to their learning characteristics. Expect highly gifted students to be finely tuned and highly aware of their differences and how others feel about them. A supportive teacher can heal wounds and build confidence. A teacher who truly challenges them is never forgotten.
- *Understand the ramifications of high levels of giftedness.* These include fast learning rate, intense personalities, and angst over poor academic and social fit—all increasing with IQ.
- *Highly gifted, twice-exceptional students should have their giftedness supported first, and their deficits accommodated second.* Teach them at the level of their reasoning. Understand that compensating for deficits is exhausting. Expect them to be late-bloomers.
- *Use teaching approaches the highly gifted love.*
    - o   Provide a classroom environment that is intellectually stimulating.
    - o   Don't try to answer all of their questions. Teach use of the Internet, computers, and library. Instruct them in how to interview, conduct polls, and speak to someone engagingly.

o Allow them to do research and present a topic to the class. Teach research skills. Trust their findings and treat them as colleagues.

o Allow them to choose study groups.

o Group them with older or other gifted students. Avoid pairing them with a struggling student or making them the "teacher's helper."

o Cut red tape to allow activities usually limited to older children.

o Don't tolerate "meanness" or bullying.

o Allow any question. Let class discussion rise to the highest level.

o Ask provocative questions that encourage thought.

o Free them from practice they don't need. Minimize homework or allow them to *apply* what they know.

o Provide lots of choices.

o Change plans if one isn't working.

o Assume their efforts will surprise you.

Conclusion: Max's Story

Twenty-year-old Max was brought for testing to rule out deficits that might explain his inconsistent performance, study and organizational skill deficiencies, and fluctuating interest in college. Tested as a child on the Stanford–Binet IV, Max earned an extraordinary IQ score of 156, documenting strengths in all areas and a strong likelihood of abilities well beyond the ceiling of the test. Yet, Max's school program had followed a fairly traditional course, except for the addition of some college courses taken in high school and part-time attendance at an alternative school. His interest in learning began to decline late in elementary school, culminating with an absolute resistance to meeting high school graduation requirements. He earned his GED through the college he attended. Despite strong support from his parents, a family emphasis on responsibility and high achievement, and efforts to build in resilience, Max's school performance lagged. Yet, the handsome, articulate, and brilliant young man excelled at rugby, foreign languages, and a variety of nonschool activities.

Further testing revealed no deficits and similar test results on the Wechsler Adult Intelligence Scale, which was not surprising for the young man who earned SAT scores of 740 and

750. However, Max presented as a profoundly gifted individual with an existential crisis. He doubted his own abilities, lacked direction, and did not understand his poor college performance. What happened to Max?

Curriculum developers try to ensure instruction at each student's level; continuous progress; and enough challenging work to hone a variety of skills, develop talents, and encourage strong work habits and organization, and realistic responses to failure. For most children, such planning helps them realize their full potential. Success with meaningful work maintains their motivation to learn and builds healthy self-esteem. However, Max missed such critical growth experiences.

He had rarely been challenged in the classroom. Even now, when the occasional problem arose for which an answer was not apparent, he froze. Unable to consider it further, he concluded he must not be as intelligent as he thought. A poor grade caused him to panic—and often to drop courses. Asked by the tester how he studied in college, he replied, "You mean read a book before a test? Never did it. Never needed to." He had no particular strategies for keeping track of assignments and missed turning in enough of them to lower his grades. He honestly did not know what caused his difficulties. "What is wrong with me?" he asked. At one point, Max considered suicide, lacking confidence that he could turn things around. His motivation was compromised; he wanted to leave school. Only for brief periods had school helped him learn or shape his extraordinary capabilities, and now he could not even succeed there.

How can opportunities for relevant instruction and meaningful accomplishment be created for a student so asynchronous? Max would have particularly benefited from radical acceleration and older classmates, beginning quite early, as Miraca Gross' (2004b) research suggests. He would have flourished in advanced classes, the challenge well within his reach and a strong motivator. Work would have been difficult enough to require the development of organizational skills while still a child. Max would have learned to try difficult problems again, breaking them into parts or considering them from other viewpoints. He might even have distinguished himself in one or two subject areas relevant to a future career. With school providing real satisfaction, Max could have faced his future life choices with confidence and a solid educational foundation.

Life choices are complicated for individuals who have the potential to do almost anything. Underachievement complicates them further. For highly gifted students as disheartened as Max, finding a new appreciation for education may take years and a variety of life experiences. As he samples the jobs he qualifies for, views the ones out of reach, and hears the occasional, "You're way too smart for this job; you need to go back to school," Max likely will find his own internal motivation. When he does, he will need to have all of those critical growth experiences he missed when school was far too easy and support from those close to him in order to persevere.

Such difficulties can more easily be prevented. Highly gifted students can and do succeed in school with a variety of unusual accommodations that are relevant to their unique needs. They simply need a successful patchwork of options that allows them to stretch, pushes them to be better, develops their talents, and maintains their motivation to learn. Accelerative options are needed at various points to provide advanced instruction, placement with true peers, and to correct the problem of being well beyond the class with little or no effort. Successful accommodations for the highly gifted normalize their school experiences and allow them to enjoy the basic benefits of education, too.

Books

Davidson, J., Davidson, B., & Vanderkam, L. (2005). *Genius denied: How to stop wasting our brightest young minds.* New York: Simon & Schuster.

Gilman, B. J. (in press). *Academic advocacy for gifted children: A parent's complete guide.* Scottsdale, AZ: Great Potential Press.

Gross, M.U.M. (2004). *Exceptionally gifted children* (2nd ed.). London: RoutledgeFalmer.

Hollingworth, L. S. (1942). *Children above 180 IQ Stanford-Binet: Origin and Developments.* Yonkers-on-Hudson, NY: World Book Company.

Kay, K., Robson, D., & Brenneman, J. F. (Eds.). (2007). *High IQ kids: Collected insights, information, and personal stories from the experts.* Minneapolis, MN: Free Spirit.

Rogers, K. (2002). *Re-forming gifted education: How parents and teachers can match the program to the child.* Scottsdale, AZ: Great Potential Press.

Ruf, D. L. (2005). *Losing our minds: Gifted children left behind.* Scottsdale, AZ: Great Potential Press.

Web Sites

A Nation Deceived
http://www.nationdeceived.org
This is the comprehensive source for information on acceleration.

The Davidson Institute for Talent Development
http://www.ditd.org
This Web site describes the offerings of the Davidson Institute for Talent Development, including the GT-CyberSource library.

Gifted Development Center
http://www.gifteddevelopment.com
The source for information on assessment of the highly gifted, this Web site also offers a library of articles and addresses advocacy, gifted children with deficits, and support groups for the exceptionally and profoundly gifted.

Hoagies' Gifted Education Page
http://www.hoagiesgifted.org
This comprehensive Web site provides information for teachers, parents, and students on all levels of giftedness, including a huge reference library of articles, information about conferences, and recommended books.

Talent Searches

Duke University Talent Identification Program (Duke TIP)
http://www.tip.duke.edu

Johns Hopkins University Center for Talented Youth (CTY)
http://cty.jhu.edu

Northwestern University Center for Talent Development (CTD)

http://www.ctd.northwestern.edu

Rocky Mountain Academic Talent Search at the University of Denver

http://www.du.edu/city

Support Organizations

The Davidson Institute

http://www.ditd.org

The Davidson Institute for Talent Development's offerings are detailed here, including the Davidson Young Scholars Program, scholarship opportunities, and The Davidson Academy of Nevada (a public school).

Gifted Development Center

http://www.gifteddevelopment.com

Information is available about POGO (Parents of Gifted Offspring), an e-mail support group for parents of children with IQs 160 and above, as well as the PG Retreat, an annual get-together for such families.

References

Boolootian, R. (2005, August). *Introduction to the first symposium on assessment of the gifted: A comparison of assessment techniques in the identification of gifted learners.* Paper presented at the 16th Biennial Conference of the World Council for Gifted and Talented Children, New Orleans, LA.

Carson, D., & Roid, G. H. (2004). *Acceptable use of the Stanford-Binet Form L-M: Guidelines for the professional use of the Stanford-Binet Intelligence Scale, Third Edition (Form L-M).* Itasca, IL: Riverside.

Colangelo, N., Assouline, S. G., & Gross, M. U. M. (2004). *A nation deceived: How schools hold back America's brightest students* (Vols. 1 and 2). Iowa City, IA: The Connie Belin & Jacqueline N. Blank International Center for Gifted Education and Talent Development.

Columbus Group. (1991, July). Unpublished transcript of the meeting of the Columbus Group, Columbus, OH.

Eide, B., & Eide, F. (2006). *The mislabeled child.* New York: Hyperion.

Flanagan, D. P., & Kaufman, A. S. (2004). *Essentials of WISC-IV Assessment.* Hoboken, NJ: John Wiley & Sons.

Flynn, J. R. (1984). The mean IQ of Americans: Massive gains 1932 to 1978. *Psychological Bulletin, 95,* 29–51.

Flynn, J. R. (1987). Massive IQ gains in 14 nations: What IQ tests really measure. *Psychological Bulletin, 101,* 171–191.

Gilman, B. J. (in press). *Academic advocacy for gifted children: A parent's complete guide.* Scottsdale, AZ: Great Potential Press.

Gilman, B. J., & Falk, R. F. (2005, August). *Research-based guidelines for use of the WISC-IV in gifted assessment.* Paper presented at the World Council for Gifted Children, New Orleans, LA.

Gross, M. U. M. (2004a). *Exceptionally gifted children* (2nd ed.). London: RoutledgeFalmer.

Gross, M. U. M. (2004b). Radical acceleration. In N. Colangelo, S. G. Assouline, & M. U. M. Gross (Eds.), *A nation deceived: How schools hold back America's brightest students* (Vol. 2, pp. 87–96). Iowa City, IA: The Connie Belin & Jacqueline N. Blank International Center for Gifted Education and Talent Development.

Hately, S. (2007). Surviving in spite of it all. In K. Kay, D. Robson, & J. F. Brenneman (Eds.), *High IQ kids* (pp. 143–149). Minneapolis, MN: Free Spirit.

Meckstroth, E. (2007). Abnormally brilliant, brilliantly normal. In K. Kay, D. Robson, & J. F. Brenneman (Eds.), *High IQ kids* (pp. 311–343). Minneapolis, MN: Free Spirit.

National Association for Gifted Children. (2008). *Position statement: Use of the WISC–IV for gifted identification.* Retrieved February 12, 2008, from http://nagc.org/index.aspx?id=2455

Rimm, S. (2006, November). *Breaking the ceiling scores for profoundly gifted children using the WISC-IV.* Paper presented at the 53rd Annual Convention of the National Association for Gifted Children, Charlotte, NC.

Rimm, S., Gilman, B. J., & Silverman, L. K. (2008). Nontraditional applications of traditional testing. In J. VanTassel-Baska (Ed.), *Alternative assessment with gifted learners* (pp. 175–202). Waco, TX: Prufrock Press.

Roid, G. H. (2003a). *Stanford-Binet Intelligence Scales interpretive manual: Expanded guide to the interpretation of SB5 test results.* Itasca, IL: Riverside.

Roid, G. H. (2003b). *Stanford-Binet Intelligence Scales, Fifth Edition, Technical manual.* Itasca, IL: Riverside.

Roid, G. H., & Carson, A. (2004). Special composites scores for the SB5. *Assessment Service Bulletin No. 4.* Itasca, IL: Riverside.

Silverman, L. K. (1998). Personality and learning styles of gifted children. In J. VanTassel-Baska (Ed.), *Excellence in educating gifted & talented learners* (3rd ed., pp. 29–65). Denver, CO: Love.

Silverman, L. K. (2001). Diagnosing and treating visual perceptual issues in gifted children. *Journal of Optometric Vision Development, 32,* 153–176.

Silverman, L. K. (2002). *Upside-down brilliance: The visual-spatial learner.* Denver, CO: DeLeon.

Silverman, L. K. (2003). Social development, leadership, and gender issues. In L. K. Silverman (Ed.), *Counseling the gifted and talented* (pp. 291–327). Denver, CO: Love.

Terman, L. M., & Merrill, M. A. (1973). *Stanford-Binet Intelligence Scale: Manual for the Third Revision Form L-M.* Boston: Houghton Mifflin.

Teasdale, T. W., & Owen. D. R. (2005). A long-term rise and recent decline in intelligence test performance: The Flynn effect in reverse. *Personality and Individual Differences, 39,* 837–843.

Wasserman, J. D. (2007). *The Flynn effect in gifted samples: Status as of 2007.* Retrieved December 9, 2007, from http://www.gifteddevelopment.com/Whats_New/flynn.htm

Wechsler, D. (2003). *The WISC-IV technical and interpretive manual.* San Antonio, TX: Psychological Corporation.

Zhu, J., Cayton, T., Weiss, L., & Gabel, A. (2008). *Wechsler Intelligence Scale for Children—Fourth Edition: Technical report #7. WISC–IV Extended norms*. Retrieved February 12, 2008, from http://harcourtassessment.com/NR/rdonlyres/ C1C19227-BC79-46D9-B43C-8E4A114F7E1F/0/ WISCIV_TechReport_7.pdf

About the Author

Barbara ("Bobbie") Gilman is associate director of the non-profit Gifted Development Center, which specializes in assessment and support of "giftedness through the life cycle." She supervises testing, participates in research, is a popular speaker for parents and teachers on advocacy and classroom accommodations for the gifted, and consults with parents worldwide. Bobbie specializes in work with the highly, exceptionally, and profoundly gifted and gifted children with learning disabilities, ADHD, or underachievement issues. She holds degrees in child development and psychology, and has extensive experience testing gifted children and making educational recommendations for them. A mother of highly gifted sons, she is a veteran of gifted committees and helped create an accelerated charter middle school. She has devoted considerable time to school advocacy with her award-winning book, *Academic Advocacy for Gifted Children: A Parent's Complete Guide* (formerly *Empowering Gifted Minds: Educational Advocacy That Works*), and helping parents to document the unique instructional needs of their gifted student, find curricular options that meet the child's needs, and plan accommodations with school personnel. A recognized expert on assessment of the gifted, Bobbie also has been writing and speaking extensively on the appropriate use and scoring of the newly revised and renormed major IQ tests with gifted children. She serves on the NAGC Task Force on IQ Test Interpretation and created NAGC's official position statement on use of the WISC-IV. She continues to love to give staff development presentations for those special teachers who recognize the unusual needs of gifted students, are looking for strategies to meet them, and "change lives."